The American Dream of Tomorrow...

Table of Contents:

Introduction
Do UFOs Actually Exist?
Who Are The Reptilian Lizard People?
The New World Order
9/11 Truthers
Who Are These QAnon Wackos?
So, The Earth Is Really Flat, Right?
The Moon Landing? Was It All a Hoax?
Where Was Barack Obama Really Born?
So, Who Really Won The 2020 Election?
When Is The Zombie Apocalypse Coming?
Should You Buy A Tin Foil Hat?
Can Evil Robots Ever Become Smarter Than Humans and Take Over The World?
So, When Is The World Going To End?
Conclusion

Introduction: Hello everyone, My name is Jeff Barlett and I am the author of the book America Today… but sadly many people did not listen to me and buy my other book so I decided to write a book called The American Dream of Tomorrow... to help wake everyone up about what is going to happen in the future of America if you don't buy and read my other book.) Just kidding, This book is just pure satire about popular conspiracy theories and in this book I make fun of how dumb these conspiracy theories actually are.

I am also the creator of a website called The Barlett Online where I poke fun at conspiracy theories. I speak up against cancel culture by defending people who have been bullied and canceled by society and the mainstream media. I also post my opinions on this website so feel free to also check out my cool and interesting website and tell all your friends about it especially if they believe in some crazy conspiracy theories. Some of the articles I have put on this website are included in this book, but don't worry this book is still going to be very entertaining to read and will be well worth your money.

In this book you will learn about some crazy conspiracy theories that people actually believe in. In this book you will also hear my opinions on these crazy conspiracy theories. I also will definitely be poking fun at some of them, especially some of the theories that are so obviously full of crap like the idea of the earth being flat or the weird reptilian lizard people. So I hope you get a good laugh when reading my book and please encourage your wired conspiracy theorist friend to purchase a copy of my book because I know they will for sure get a good kick out of this one. Hopefully after reading this book all your crazy conspiracy theory believing friends can finally take off their funny tin foil hat.

Do UFOs Actually Exist?

So do you actually believe that UFOs exist? Well you are not alone, because there are many other crazy weirdos just like you who actually believe in the same thing. If you ever been through Roswell, New Mexico you will notice how the town is decorated with alien stuff to attract tourists because of these popular conspiracy theories. Also don't forget about those area 51 conspiracy theories as well that people actually believe in. But because there are so many UFO conspiracy theories out there I decided to make one up for you all to prove to you all how easily conspiracy theories get spread around on the internet. I hope you all won't be dumb enough to belive in this one.

Since I live in Apache Junction, Arizona and there are alot of crazy rednecks who live in my town who believe in some of the craziest conspiracy theories, let's make this event take place in Apache Junction. So hey everyone, Did you all hear about The UFO that was spotted in Apache Junction, Arizona last night. It was a very interesting view. So here is an article I decided to write on my website about The UFO encounter in Apache Junction, Arizona.

*Here is My Article From The Barlett Online About The UFO Encounter in Apache Junction?

"So hello everyone, Did you hear the news about The UFO sighting in Apache Junction, Arizona last night. Did you notice anyone missing because they have been abducted by aliens? It was a very interesting experience to encounter extraterrestrial life. We even got some proof to post it online and share it all over social media for everyone to see for themselves. Some people even believe that this is a reptilian elite group of aliens who abducted everyone last night. I was so worried they might even take me with them, and I had a very strange dream last night where I was in space and was able to see real live aliens with a reptilian-like appearance. They even told me about their crazy plan to create a one world government and about how they are the ones really in control of our world economy. It was definitely a very interesting experience to encounter. I hope they don't come for you next time.

Well everyone, Do you believe me or do you think I am just full of crap like any other wacko when telling you this story. I would hope that you would think that I am full of crap for telling you this story, not because of the *unlikeliness of this ever happening and the fact that there are so many crazy conspiracy theories out there on the internet just like this one, but because I just made this story up to prove a point to you all how easily conspiracy theories get spread around on the internet. And the picture you see in the article is NOT even from Apache Junction, Arizona but is a public domain photo that was taken in Passaic, New Jersey in 1952 most likely of a blimp or similar looking aircraft in the sky. But there are many people willing to jump to conclusions and say it was aliens because of course that will make a great headline for a conspiracy theorist news website. What is really interesting is NOT the fact that there are so many conspiracy theorists out there in the world who are just looking for ways to drive traffic to their websites to make some money, but the fact that there are so many idiots in the world who actually believe in this kind of nonsense. I hope you all enjoy reading my fun and interesting article and thank you for reading, and God Bless..."*

I hope you enjoyed reading this article which I actually posted on my website called barlettonline.com where I poke fun at a bunch of crazy conspiracy theories just like this one. These kinds of articles are intended to make people laugh at the stupidity of some of these crazy conspiracy theories.

Who Are The Reptilian Lizard People?

So did you know that there are some weirdos in this world who actually believe the world is being controlled by The Reptilian Lizard People? How Interesting? You may have noticed me using the idea of reptilian lizard people in my crazy UFO article because usually these reptilian conspiracy theorists are likely to also believe in UFO encounter conspiracy theories as well as their own crazy reptilian conspiracy theories.

So if you actually believe that our government is controlled by some reptilian lizard people I got a fun experiment for you to try. Do some research on how this conspiracy theory was started and you will start to wonder if the guy was just making this one up for some publicity like what most conspiracy theorists do. Also if reprillians actually were running things don't you think that they might have come after you by now for exposing their evil plans?

The New World Order

So are we going to have a one world government someday that is controlled by an elite group called the illuminati ? Are most of our politicians part of this elite group and do they all have a special hand signal they give when they give speeches on television? Does the Bible actually back up this claim or are people actually misinterpreting what the Bible actually says just like when people used to misinterpret the words of Jesus Christ when he was walking the earth during his ministry on the earth.

But some people believe that someday we will have a one world government that actually contradicts what the Bible says. If you read The Book of Daniel you will read about him interpreting Nebuchadnezzar's dream and this dream does not even speak of a one world government at the end but of a divided kingdom. Also another thing I find very funny is that people will worry about higher us in the so-called illuminati but then they voted for Donald Trump. Would you not think that former President Trump is part of this elite system if it existed?

9/11 Truthers

The attacks on The World Trade Center was a tragic event that resulted in the loss of many people. And sometimes tragedy is followed by some crazy conspiracy theories. Some people actually don't believe that 9/11 was caused by the terrorist but was an inside job done by our own government.

Some of these people will even fold up their $20 bills to try to make an illusion of the twin towers burning. So if you are one of these people I would highly encourage you to read the section about these crazy $20 bill conspiracy theories. If that does not convince you maybe you can try to convince me with my challenge I made for you where you send me your $20 bills so I can examine them myself. Disclaimer I wont refund your money if you are actually dumb enougth to try this challage.

So, Do You Believe In These Crazy $20 Bill Conspiracy Theories?

So since there are plenty of crazy $20 bill conspiracy theories out there on the internet I decided to make a challenge for these wackos who believe in these wacky conspiracy theories. The challenge is for them to send me their folded $20 bills so I can examine their bills for myself and I even included a disclaimer in my challenge that I won't refund their money to them if they are dumb enough to try this challage. Then of course I decided to post the challenge on social media but I couldn't find anyone who was actually actually willing to take on this challenge. So maybe people are just full of crap with their crazy conspiracy theories.)

*So Here is my challenge I made to these crazy $20 bill conspiracy theorists that I put in an article on my website and posted to social media.

"Did you know that some people will even fold $20 bills to try to prove their point with some of these crazy *theories. Some people will actually fold their $20 bills to make an illusion of the world trade center or the illusion of a woman wearing a mask with the numbers saying 2020. And did you know that 9 plus eleven actually equals 20? If you are that good at math you probably then maybe you need someone to help manage your money for you. Maybe you should try my fun experiment I created for you.*

Please keep reading... Well, maybe these people should also put their $20 bills in an envelope and send it to me so I can see it for myself. I sure wonder how many of these people will never see their $20 bill again after they try this cool experiment, but don't worry it would be a very fun experiment to try.) And don't worry I won't ever refund your money to you so you can definitely trust me with your folded $20 bills. I will probably use it to go on some spending spree for you all.)) So if you believe in these crazy conspiracy theories then maybe you should try my cool and fun experiment and see if you can convince me to believe in your crazy conspiracy theories;) And if you can pull this experiment with $100 you might actually have a slight chance of convincing me to believe in some of your crazy conspiracy theories. So what are you waiting for? What do you have to lose? Except for $20 of course, and $100 if you are really that smart to send it over to me.) But if you are wise enough to believe in some of these conspiracy theories then you would be very wise to send me some of your money as well.) If not, then you should really think about what kind of nonsense you are *actually believing in. Thank you for reading and God*

Bless...

Disclaimer: I won't refund your money if you are dumb

enough to try this challenge."

Who Are These QAnon Wackos?

So according to these QAnon conspiracy theorist we live in a world that is controlled by a buch of satanic cannibalistic pedophiles who are running a global sex trafficing ring. And most of the Hollywood stars are even involved in this, and that is why Hollywood and The media hate Donald Trump, Right? Some of these crazies think that Donald Trump is still the President and that Biden did not win the 2020 Presidential election. I sure wonder if we can really believe in this one? Right?))

So, The Earth Is Really Flat, Right?

I find it very interesting that there are many people in the world who actually believe that the earth is flat. Of course if there are people who are able to make a ton of money off of a flat earther convention then there will be plenty of flat earth conspiracy theorists and some crazy followers who actually believe in these weird theories. These wackos even have their own map of their crazy flat earth ideas and they actually believe that Antarctica is at the edge of the earth. Some of these flat earthers will actually get up in an airplane and not look out at the horizon but use their bogus device to try to prove their crazy conspiracy theories to be true.

I would highly encourage the flat earthers to take a trip in an airplane and notice how the mountains are not flat, and if you ever get to fly in a commercial airplane that flies at supersonic speeds you might actually be able to see the earth's curvature. If you get up in an airplane and fly in the same direction from New York, to London, Then to Moscow, then to Tokyo, then to Los Angeles, then back to New York then you literally just flew around the world and ended up right back where you started by flying only east so you may be wondering how is this even possible? Well, the earth was made in a sphere-like shape so you were able to fly around the world without ever even flying west to end up back where you started. And most airlines are even smart enough to route their flights North so they can save a ton of money on fuel and not have to route longer flights over the ocean. If the world was actually flat then this would be impossible to achieve and your airline tickets would be much more expensive. Thankfully due to a round earth we can fly around the world for much less.

But since all you flat earthers like to come up with your own maps, I got another fun experiment for you all to try. Get 2 ships one in Southwest Harbor, Maine and the other ship in Miami Florida. What you are going to want to do is at the same time sail both of your ships to Africa and see who will get their first. If you are actually dumb enough to actaully waste your hard earned money trying this experiment then you will start to wonder why the ship from Maine actually made it to Africa before the ship from Miami and that is because the earth is round and Maine is actually closer to Africa then Florida is so all you flat earthers actually learned something new today. I hope all you flat earthers spent a good time studying geography when you design your next flat earther map.

Another thing you can do is take a ride on a ship and sail around the globe. One thing you will be able to notice is that if you start in New York City, then sail to London, Then you sail up north past the coastlines of Sweden and Russia you will eventually make your way to Wales, Alaska. Yes, I said it's Alaska but let's keep going if you don't believe me let's keep sailing up north following the Alaska coastline and through the Arctic ocean with your new ice breaker ship because regular ships will have a hard time up here all the way to Nova Scotia, Canada. Now you probably think that you are actually getting really close to just falling off a big waterfall, but wait all you need to do is sail down south across the coastlines on the Atlantic Ocean and you are right back in New York City where you started your journey wondering how this was even possible. Well, the answer is the earth is a big round sphere and your crazy flat earth conspiracy theories are nothing but a crazy myth.

Did you know that some of these flat earthers will even try to use the Bible to back up their claims, but wait the Bible actually says the opposite of what these flat earthers actually claim. Here is also a Bible verse that I personally feel that these flat earthers should be reading. So maybe all you flat earthers out there should do some research and you will learn how the earth is actually round and not flat. Please read the Bible verse below.

Job 26:7
King James Version
7 He stretcheth out the north over the empty place, and hangeth the earth upon nothing.

The Moon Landing? Was It All a Hoax?

So this is probably one of the first conspiracy theories that I have ever heard of. I remember when I was in the 9th grade my science teacher wanted us all to pick an important event from outer space and do a research project on it. Guess what event I picked? I decided to do a research project on How The Moon Landing Was A Hoax because I thought it was funny and it would make me look cool in front of the entire class. Thankfully for me, my science teacher was actually on board with this one because he actually was really cool. I sure wonder what would have happened if I pulled off a stunt like this with another teacher? Hopefully they wouldn't be too emotionally sensitive about my cool and interesting content;)

So now let's talk about this popular conspiracy theory. Did you know that there are people who actually believe in the idea that the moon landing was all a hoax? I even have seen videos on the internet with many interesting claims that people make to try to prove their point to get you to believe in their conspiracy theories. Some people will show video footage of the american flag moving while in space, but there's no wind in space right? Unless of course the flag is moving because the astronauts are moving the flag around. But, hey, we can make edits to camera footage and spread some crazy conspiracy theories about how man never walked on the moon. I sure wonder if we ever walked on the planet Earth and are not actually living on the Mars if people are crazy enough to believe in this one.))

Where Was Barack Obama Really Born?

So was President Barack Obama actually born in Kenya? Or is this just another conspiracy theory created by well known conspiracy theorist Donald Trump.

Did you know that before Donald Trump was President he actually made a challenge that if President Obama was able to release a copy of his birth certificate that he would donate 5 million dollars to a charity of his choice. President Obama was able to provide a copy of his birth certificate and it proves that he was born in Honolulu, Hawaii so I think President Donald Trump might actually owe President Obama 5 millions dollars to a charity of his choice. So maybe Donald Trump should pay up.

So, Who Really Won The 2020 Election?

Did Donald Trump really win the 2020 election? Is Donald Trump really The President of The United States and we are all just crazy for believing that Joe Biden actually won and is currently in The Oval Office as President of The United States?

This also reminds me of The 2000 election between George Bush and Al Gore where Florida was the deciding factor on who got to become President. And of course they were not able to overturn this one, and if we did have the ability to overturn an election due to election fraud; Then does that mean Al Gore should get to be President for 4 years to help clean things up before Donald Trump makes another mess?

What people need to realize is that you can't just overturn an election like that because someone claims there is voter fraud without having due process. It would actually be a violation of our liberties if this actually happened. Also people need to understand that we as citizens don't even vote directly for our President like we do for other offices. We actually vote for electors in the electoral college and they actually vote directly for The President. The system was designed this way for a reason. To prevent things like what we saw in the 2020 election from happening. If you want to know more about The electoral college please read The U.S. Constitution. Hopefully people will someday realize that you can't just overturn the will of the people in an election just because they don't like the outcome of the results.

When Is The Zombie Apocalypse Coming?

So since there are so many people who believe in the idea of a zombie apocalypse, probably because they play too many video games and watch too many zombie apocalypse movies I am going to write about this crazy conspiracy theory. If you actually believe in such fantasies like this one I am already assuming that your brains were already eaten out by the zombies by now. But since all these video games and zombie movies are so popular these days, I felt that I just had to include the idea of a zombie apocalypse in my book for anyone who is crazy enough to actually believe that this one is true. Hopefully I did not offend anyone by including this section into my book.)

Should You Buy A Tin Foil Hat?

So you may be wondering if you should buy a tin foil hat. Well if I am the guy selling it to you for a crazy amount of money then sure, Why Not? But if you are some wacko who believes in some crazy conspiracy theories, maybe you should get yourself a tin foil hat so people can easily identify you as some crazy conspiracy theorist so they know not to take any of your bogus claims seriously.

But since we are discussing tin foil hats let me tell you all about this crazy conspiracy theory. Did you know that there are actually some weirdos out there who actually believe that their tin foil hats will protect them from government mind control. If you don't believe me, look this one up for yourself. These hats are so how designed very well to the point where it actually shields your dumb little brain from threats like mind control, electromagnetic fields, and and from any kind of mind reading. But don't worry if you wear one of these hats in public people will actually think you are a genius.

So I got a fun challenge for all you tin foil hat wearing conspiracy theorists out there. Maybe you should apply for a job as a college professor and wear your wacky tin foil hat to the job interview. I am pretty sure this will help you stand out very well from the other job applicants who want to become a professor at the university. If you happen to get rejected by the university then maybe you should try applying for a job at your local circus. They would probably love to have you there. Or maybe you can try giving the university some of your hard earned money and they might actually take the time to school you on why your tin foil hat conspiracy theories are just pure nonsense. But if you want to try this experiment then I hope you have fun.

Can Evil Robots Ever Become Smarter Than Humans and Take Over The World?

Well, I think this one has already happened because if people are dumb enough to belive in some crazy conspiracy theories on the internet, then they are probaby dumb enough not to realize that they are already not smarter then their average computer.

But did you know that some weirdos actually believe that evil robots will become so advanced someday that they will eventually become smarter than humans and take over the world? Wow, because if people are actually dumb enough to believe in this nonsence then maybe the evil robot computers are actaully in fact already smarter then most humans.

So, When Is The World Going To End?

So I remember when I was a kid the world was supposed to end on December 21, 2012 which was also the end of The Mayan calendar. But why are we still here? I thought the world was supposed to end on December 21, 2012 or maybe it is supposed to happen on New Year's Day in the year 2000 so we all better party like it's 1999 because once the clock hits midnight on Y2K we are going to experience some crazy disasters.

What year do you believe the world is going to end? Let me tell you all what I believe. I personally believe in what the Bible says and what is written in the Bible is that no man knoweth the day or the hour so all these weirdos who like to make predictions on when the world is going to end are wrong. My challenge for you is to actually read the Bible cover to cover and see for yourself what the Bible says and when your preacher starts preaching politics telling you how the world is going to end, look up the scripture reference in the Bible and show it directly to them.

Another thing you can do is run out in the streets with a sign saying doomsday is near and make sure you are wearing your tin foil hat so people all know who you really are. You can also post some pictures of yourself with your tinfoil hat and doomsday sign on social media so people can get a good laugh at you when you become a viral meme for your doomsday conspiracy theories. Another thing you can do is get on your computer and do some actual research on these doomsday conspiracy theories and realize that people thought the world was going to end for thousands of years so what makes you so special for your new conspiracy theory.

Another thing you can do is research some history. You can learn about how everyone thought the world was going to end in the year 2000 because of Y2K which was when people were so worried about computers crashing. You can do some research on The December 21, 2012 conspiracy theory when people thought the world was going to end because this was the end of the mayan calendar. Or in 1910 people were worried about the world ending because Halley's Comet was appearing in the sky as it usually does about every 75 years. But if you actually think the world is going to end soon, then maybe you should do some research on some of these crazy conspiracy theories and ask yourself this question. Why in the world are we still here?

Conclusion

Well I hope you enjoyed reading my book The American Dream of Tomorrow... about some of the craziest conspiracy theories that people actually believe in here in America. If you enjoyed reading my book, please tell all your friends about my book, especially if you have any crazy conspiracy theory believing friends who think everything is a big conspiracy. They will definitely get a kick out of reading this book. Maybe my book will school them and give them some brains and some common sense to not believe in such crazy conspiracy theories. Hopefully the real The American Dream of Tomorrow... does not look like any of these crazy conspiracy theories that are portrayed in this book. I would like to thank you all for reading my book. Thank You and God Bless...